TEN THOUSAND BUDDHAS CITY
ACCOMPLISHES
TEN THOUSAND BUDDHAS

Pearls of Wisdom by The Venerable Master Hua

萬佛城

萬佛成

宣化上人衣裏明珠 5

萬佛城・萬佛成
Thousand Buddhas City accomplishes Ten Thousand Buddhas

萬佛城・萬佛成
Ten Thousand Buddhas City accomplishes Ten Thousand Buddhas

Published and translated by:
Buddhist Text Translation Society
1777 Murchison Drive
Burlingame, CA 94010-4504
www.drba.org

2010 Buddhist Text Translation Society
Dharma Realm Buddhist University
Dharma Realm Buddhist Association

15 14 13 12 11 10   10 9 8 7 6 5 4 3 2 1

Printed in Taiwan

ISBN: 978-0-88139-869-4

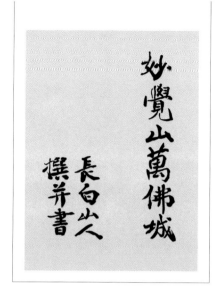

妙覺山萬佛城

長白山人 撰并書

編案：1980年代宣公上人更名「萬佛城」為「萬佛聖城」，
本書為保持上人開示時的口語，一律以「萬佛城」稱之。

Editor's note: in the 1980s, the Venerable Master Hua changed the
name of the "City of Ten Thousand Buddhas" to the "Sagely City of
Ten Thousand Buddhas." However, in order to preserve accuracy
of the Venerable Master's talks prior to this change, the City 'is
referred to as the "City of Ten Thousand Buddhas" throughout this
book.

妙覺世尊等覺菩薩千百億化身變海為山

The Flower Adornment Dharma Assembly,
the Shurangama Platform,
and the Forty-two Hands and Eyes
establish the Heavens and the Earth.

The World Honored Ones of Wonderful Enlightenment
and the Bodhisattvas of Equal Enlightenment,
with a billion Transformation bodies,
can turn oceans into mountains.

華嚴法會楞嚴壇場四十二手眼安天立地

西方佛法露曙光
東度眾生壽而康
悟得本來無生面
與爾同登萬佛邦

In the West, the Buddhadharma radiates a bright light of dawn,
As in the East, it rescues beings and bestows long life and health.
If you can awaken to the truth that originally there is no birth or death,
On the spot, you can ascend together to Ten Thousand Buddhalands.

我們現在是開闢新天地，
在這個世界上把佛教的種子，
種在每一粒微塵裏邊；
每一粒微塵裏邊，我們都要在那兒轉大法輪，弘揚佛法。
這個工作，是我們每一個人的責任，不是其他人的責任。
我們做佛教徒就應該做佛教的事情，
把佛教推行到每一粒微塵裏邊去，每一個世界去，
推而廣之到整個法界裏邊去，這是我們應該做的工作！

Now we are breaking new ground by planting the seed of Buddhadharma in every single dust particle. And in every single dust particle, we turn the great Dharma Wheel and propagate the Buddhadharma. The responsibility of this work belongs to each one of us, and cannot be left to anyone else. As disciples of the Buddha, we should do the Buddha's work by extending the Dharma to every single particle of dust and to every world system, until it fills the entire Dharma Realm. This is work that we ought to do!

萬佛城，
這不是一萬尊佛才叫萬佛城，
而是一尊佛也叫萬佛城，
一萬尊佛也叫萬佛城，
萬萬尊佛還是叫萬佛城；
這萬萬就是無窮無盡的，
這都叫萬佛城。
誰來了，誰就有份成佛，
到了萬佛城，將來是一定要成佛的；
你若不想成佛，就來不到萬佛城。
我們這個萬佛城，
也是諸佛為大家來大做佛事預備的。

The "City of Ten Thousand Buddhas" did not get its name because there are ten thousand Buddhas here. The name remains the same regardless of whether there is one Buddha, ten thousand Buddhas, or one hundred million Buddhas. The number "ten thousand" represents infinity. Whoever comes to the City of Ten Thousand Buddhas has the ability to become a Buddha. If you come here, you will be a Buddha in the future. However, if you do not want to become a Buddha, then you should not come. Moreover, the City of Ten Thousand Buddhas also has been prepared by a myriad of Buddhas to enable all of us to do the Buddha's work.

成立萬佛城這個因緣，

可以說在無量劫以來就注定的，

注定佛法要傳到西方來，

所以時候到了，萬佛城就出現了。

這個出現，不是從天上掉下來，

也不是從地上湧出來的，而是人造出來的，

造出來七、八十棟房子。

這七、八十棟房子怎麼造成的？

因為在第二次世界大戰以前，是美國最有錢的時候，

所以才能建起這樣規模的房子；

這些房子，都沒有偷工減料，實打實著，很堅固的，

所用的材料也特別好。

The causes and conditions for establishing the City of Ten Thousand Buddhas were determined limitless eons ago. It was determined then that the Buddhadharma would be propagated to the West, and when that time came, the City of Ten Thousand Buddhas would appear. However, the City did not make its appearance by falling down from the heavens or by welling forth from the earth. Rather, it was built by people. Seventy to eighty buildings were constructed here. How did these buildings come into being?

They were constructed before WWII, during a period of great affluence in America. That is why a complex of such magnitude could be built. These buildings were not constructed shoddily with inferior materials. Rather, they are very sturdy because they were constructed with honest labor and materials of especially high quality.

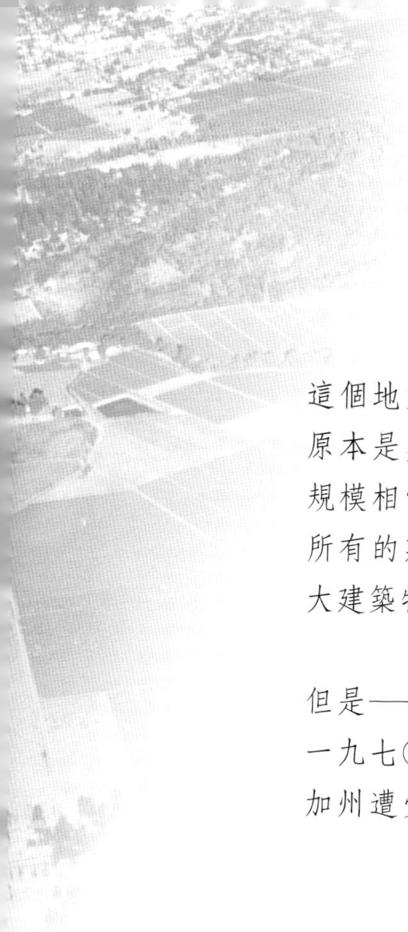

這個地方，在一九三〇年代開始啓建，
原本是美國加州州政府興建的公立療養院，
規模相當宏大，
所有的建築物和內部設備都是一流的。
大建築物有七十餘座，大小房間二千餘間…。

但是——
一九七〇年代中期，
加州遭受到史無前例的大旱災……

Originally a large state hospital complex built by the California government was located on this site. Its construction started in the 1930s, and all of its buildings and facilities were first rate. There were over seventy large buildings and two thousand rooms of various sizes.... However, in the mid-1970s, California suffered a drought of unprecedented severity.

所以房子造好了，或者也沒有錢了，
加上從前這裏有病人和工作人員約六千人，
耗水量很大，這一切的開銷還了得！
這個地方的水源非常困難，
附近地區盡是果園，處處需要水，
所以果園園主常向政府訴怨，
反對公家的事業和民間爭水，
這也是不得不關閉的大原因。
因為沒有水，所以也不能開伙了，
水火不能濟濟——
水不幫助火了，火也不能幫助水了；
人不能幫助水了，水也不能幫助人了。
在這個情形之下，政府就要把它賣了…

It was possible that the hospital did not have any funds left after the completion of its construction. In addition, as there were around 6,000 patients and hospital workers living here, the water consumption must have been quite high and other expenses must have been considerable as well. In addition, water is very scarce in this area, and there were a lot of nearby orchards and vineyards that also needed water. Indeed, the owners of neighboring orchards often brought their grievances to the local government, voicing their opposition against a public institution's competition with the local people for water. This was another reason that the hospital was forced to close. Since there was no water, people could not even cook their meals. Two of the Five Elements, water and fire, were unable to provide mutual aid - the water could not help the fire, and the fire could not help the water. Similarly, people could not help the water, and the water could not help people. Under these circumstances, the government decided to sell the property.

那時在舊金山的金山寺雖然有三層樓，
面積共有一萬八千平方呎，
可是法會的時候，人一多起來，也不夠用。
我有個徒弟，出家之後，想幫師父做點事，
就各處去找地方。他從北邊回來，路經這所醫院，
一看這個地方要出賣，就請我去看看。

我就帶五個弟子去看，一看！這麼好的地方，
這麼多房子，價錢這麼貴，怎麼辦呢？
別說我一個窮和尚，就是一個萬金和尚也買不起，
所以連想也不敢想，更不要說買啊！

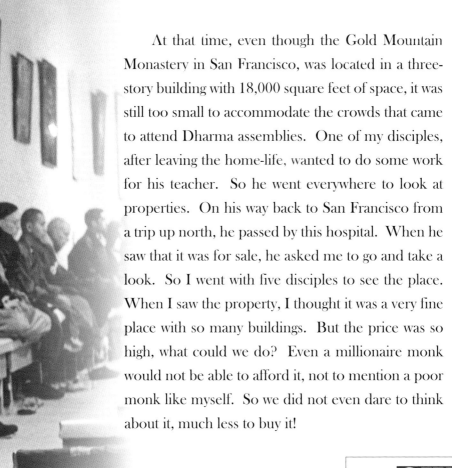

At that time, even though the Gold Mountain Monastery in San Francisco, was located in a three-story building with 18,000 square feet of space, it was still too small to accommodate the crowds that came to attend Dharma assemblies. One of my disciples, after leaving the home-life, wanted to do some work for his teacher. So he went everywhere to look at properties. On his way back to San Francisco from a trip up north, he passed by this hospital. When he saw that it was for sale, he asked me to go and take a look. So I went with five disciples to see the place. When I saw the property, I thought it was a very fine place with so many buildings. But the price was so high, what could we do? Even a millionaire monk would not be able to afford it, not to mention a poor monk like myself. So we did not even dare to think about it, much less to buy it!

凍死不攀緣　餓死不化緣　窮死不求緣　隨緣不變　不變隨緣

捨命為佛事　造命為本事　革命為僧事　即事

這樣過了半年，又來了一個人和我商量，
說可以投資作生意，可是我也沒有本錢。
雖然如此，我還是和十八個人到那個地方，
先看位於前面的一棟醫院，看了，心也就動了，
心想：「單單造這棟醫院也造不出來！」
所以我就和一起去的十八個弟子提起，
我說：「我們都是佛教徒，應該為佛教徒做點事情，
如果我們沒有為佛教徒做事情，
應該生大慚愧，沒有什麼面目見世間人；
所以今天我要發願，要把所有的房子和土地買下來！」

After half a year, someone came and negotiated with me, suggesting that I purchase the hospital as an investment. However, I did not have enough funds, let alone capital for investment. Despite this, I still took 18 people to take a look at the place again. I first looked at the clinic building located at the front of the property. When I saw the building, I thought, "After spending so much money, they could not even manage to finish constructing the clinic." I then turned to the others and said, "We are all disciples of the Buddha, and we should do something on behalf of Buddhism. If we fail to do so, we should be greatly ashamed of ourselves. We will not be able to hold up our heads before the world. Therefore, today, I am making a vow to buy the entire property with all its buildings and land!"

各位想一想，以我這一個窮和尚來講，
也沒有什麼很有錢的護法，
居然能把世界人所不能做的事情做了
——將萬佛城建立起來。
在這麼一個末法時代，
能有這麼樣一個大的道場從地湧出，
可以說是天造地設的，
給我們預備一座現成的道場。

Everyone, just think about this. I am a poor monk and do not have very rich lay supporters. Yet, incredibly, I managed to accomplish something that no one else in the world could do -- the founding of the City of Ten Thousand Buddhas. In this Dharma-ending Age, when a Way-place of this scale emerged from the ground, it was the culmination of the causes and conditions that would enable a Way-place to be readily available for us.

於是我們到這兒，
可以很容易地成就這一座大的道場，
並且正在辦一所大學，
造就世界真正有良心道德，
知道怎麼樣做人的這種人，
這真是不可思議！
我們以這個不可思議的境界來觀察觀察，
這要不是十方三世一切諸佛
來幫著我們大做佛事，
怎麼能有這樣的成就？
所以大家應該明白，
這就是佛示現這麼大一個道場，
讓我們所有的人在這兒用功修行。

Therefore, it is really inconceivable that we could easily build this big Way-place, and also be in the process of establishing a university where we can train students with a genuine sense of righteousness, morality and humaneness! If we examine this inconceivable state, how could we have accomplished such a feat without the Buddhas of the ten directions and three periods of time helping us to do the great work of a Buddha? So we should understand that the Buddhas manifested such a large Way-place so that everyone could come here to cultivate diligently.

現在佛教在西方初露曙光,
不要把它變成末法時代,
一定要令正法常住於世。
什麼是正法住世?
你老老實實去修行,
不好虛名假利,不貪供養,就是正法住世。
如果每個出家人,能持銀錢戒,能坐禪,
能日中一食,能時刻搭袈裟,嚴持戒律,
就是正法住世,也就是依佛所教,躬行實踐。

At this time, when Buddhism is just beginning to dawn in the West, do not turn it into the Dharma-ending Age. The Proper Dharma must certainly dwell long in the world. What does it mean for the Proper Dharma to dwell in the world? If you cultivate honestly without craving fame, profit, or offerings, then the Proper Dharma is dwelling in the world. If every Sangha member upholds the precept of not touching money, sits in Chan meditation, eats one meal a day at noon, wears the precept sash at all times, and upholds the precepts strictly, then the Proper Dharma is dwelling in the world. We should put the Buddha's teachings into actual practice.

若想對佛法有所幫助，就要真正弘揚佛法，
以身作則，注意四大威儀，持守五戒，
用慈悲喜捨四無量心來度眾生，
用不爭、不貪、不求、不自私、不自利、不妄語
這六大宗旨，為律己的準繩。
用這樣的法則去推行佛法，
無論在什麼時候都是正法，不會有末法出現。

If you want to help Buddhism, you have to actually propagate the Buddhadharma, set a good example for others, maintain good deportment, keep the five precepts, and save living beings by means of the four limitless minds of kindness, compassion, joy, and giving. Our conduct should be based upon the Six Guiding Principles of not fighting, not being greedy, not seeking, not being selfish, not pursuing personal advantage, and not lying. If we practice the Buddhadharma according to these guidelines, then the Proper Dharma will be present wherever we are. The decline of the Dharma will not manifest.

萬佛城是正法住世的一座城，
有了萬佛城，
天魔外道都恐怖毛豎，旁門左道戰戰兢兢，
令他們都寢不安息，食不甘味，
時時刻刻都想把萬佛城消滅了，
令它不成功，可是這沒有用的！
萬佛城是由十方諸佛共同擁護的一座道場，
所以萬佛城現在在這個地球上，
是一座正法開始的道場，
是一座從來未有的正法道場！

The City of Ten Thousand Buddhas is where the Proper Dharma dwells. After the founding of this City, the demons and heretical teachers are in such terror that their hair stands on end. The followers of the unorthodox ways are also trembling with fear. They cannot sleep well or enjoy their food. They are constantly trying to figure out how to destroy the City, how to cause it to fail. However, their efforts are useless! The City of Ten Thousand Buddhas is a Way-place protected and supported by the Buddhas of the ten directions. Therefore, right now on this Earth, the City of Ten Thousand Buddhas is a Way-place where the Proper Dharma begins. It is a Way-place of the Proper Dharma never seen before

所以我們這兒打地藏七、打觀音七，或者打佛七、打禪七，
都是特別辛苦的，沒有休息的時間；
因為你要是想休息，就不能修道；
你要是想修道，就不能休息。
你要是貪自在，又想貪享受，又想成佛，
是沒有這個道理的，沒有說是樣樣都是我佔便宜的。
我們萬佛城知道這一點，
所以人人都要苦幹來用功修行，真正發菩提心；
不要一天到晚盡打妄想，盡想去攀緣，
盡想去和任何人拉攏什麼關係；
凡是到萬佛城來的人，對這一點都應該認得清清楚楚。
因此在萬佛城的人，人人都應努力擁護這個道場。

Here, when we hold Earthstore Bodhisattva Sutra Recitation Sessions, Gwan Yin Bodhisattva Recitation Sessions, Amitabha Buddha Recitation Sessions, and Chan Meditation Sessions, we work very hard, with no time to rest. That is because if you want to rest, you cannot cultivate. Conversely, if you want to cultivate, you cannot rest. There is no way if you are greedy for comfort and enjoyment that you can become a Buddha. There is no shortcut to Buddhahood. We at the City of Ten Thousand Buddhas understand this point. Therefore, everyone must cultivate diligently, with a willingness to toil and suffer, and truly bring forth the Bodhi resolve. Do not engage in idle thinking all day long, such as thinking about getting things and how to establish relationships with people who may benefit you. Everyone who comes to the City of Ten Thousand Buddhas has to be clear about this. Therefore, everyone at the City of Ten Thousand Buddhas should diligently support and protect this Way-place.

在美國這個國家，
佛教是一個開始，開始一定要有一個基礎；
若沒有基礎，佛教是不會發揚光大的。
基礎在什麼地方呢？基礎就要從教育上著手。
所以我們萬佛城設有育良小學、培德中學、
法界佛教大學，還有僧伽居士訓練班。
小學的宗旨是盡孝道，
中學就要盡忠為國，大學就講仁義道德；
以上是我們小學、中學、大學
要維新改良社會教育一個簡略的總觀念，
而僧伽居士訓練班就是要培育造就佛教人才。
我們辦教育，教育出人才，可以翻譯經典，可以講經說法。

Buddhism is just starting in America, and it needs a good foundation, because without a good foundation, Buddhism will not flourish. So how can we lay a good foundation? It begins with education. Therefore, at the City of Ten Thousand Buddhas we have Instilling Goodness Elementary School, Developing Virtue Secondary School, Dharma Realm Buddhist University, and the Sangha and

Laity Training Programs. In the elementary school, education is based on developing filial piety; the secondary school emphasizes how to be good citizens; and, the University focuses on the virtues of humaneness, righteousness, and morality. The foregoing is just a general concept of how our schools aim at improving and reforming the education system in society. The Sangha and Laity Training Programs provide training for people who aspire to pursue careers in Buddhism. Through education, we can produce talented individuals who are capable of translating the Sutras and lecturing on the Buddhadharma.

現在在美國這兒發揚佛教，
這不是說哪一個國家的，這是世界性的。
將來你們都要到世界各處去弘揚佛法，
所以現在要造就人才。
造就人才，一定要有基礎，
所以現在就要創立一座大道場，
作為世界佛教的一個基礎。
因為這樣各位都要努力，不要懶惰，
這件事在這兒的每個人，人人都有份的，
我們要發心成就這座大道場。

Although we are propagating the Buddhadharma in the U.S. now, this work is not limited to a particular country. Rather, it is worldwide. In the future, you will be going all over the world to propagate the Dharma, so we need to train talented individuals now. In order to produce such individuals, there must be a good foundation, so we need to establish a large Way-place now to serve as a solid foundation for Buddhism all over the world. Because of this, everyone needs to work hard and not be lazy. It is the responsibility of everyone here to resolve to make this Way-place possible.

萬佛城過去是一個有病的人住的地方，
是一個將要死的人住的地方；
而現在是一個沒有疾病的人住的地方，
身體健康，並且想要開悟，
得到佛果菩提的人住的地方。

萬佛城怎麼來的？
萬佛城就是從我們苦幹來的，修行來的！
我們修行不能自讚譭他，說我們修行是對了，
但是我們有多少是真的，諸佛菩薩就有多大感應！

In the past, the City of Ten Thousand Buddhas was a place where the sick and the dying lived. However, now, it is the home of healthy people who wish to attain liberation and enlightenment. How did the City of Ten Thousand Buddhas come about? It is the result of our tremendous effort and cultivation. When we cultivate, we should not praise ourselves and criticize others, claiming that the way we cultivate is the right one. Depending on how sincere we are, the myriad Buddhas and Bodhisattvas will respond accordingly.

在萬佛城發心的人將來都一定成佛的，
我們不做三十三天的天主，
也不做三十四天、三十五天的天主，
我們一定要成萬佛，在萬佛城成萬佛！
劉果濟居士以前寫了一首打油詩：

萬佛城中萬佛生　萬丈光芒萬戶燈
萬眾一心萬代業　萬邦共仰萬佛城

所以所有來萬佛城的人，都是萬佛之中的一份子；
不但萬佛，而是無邊佛、無數佛、無等佛，
也就是不可說佛、那由他佛，
所以這些不可思議的佛，
都要從這兒發菩提心出現於世的。

Anyone who brings forth the Bodhi resolve at the City of Ten Thousand Buddhas will definitely become a Buddha in the future. We are not interested in being the Lords of the Thirty-third, Thirty-fourth, or Thirty-fifth Heavens. We are determined to become ten thousand Buddhas. After all, at the City of Ten Thousand Buddhas, ten thousand beings come to accomplish Buddhahood. Upasaka Liu Gwo Ji wrote the following verse of encouragement:

> *In the City of Ten Thousand Buddhas,*
> *   ten thousand Buddhas are born.*
> *Ten thousand miles of bright light shines forth*
> *   from the lamps of ten thousand households.*
> *With one mind, ten thousand people do the great work*
> *   that will last for ten thousand generations.*
> *Ten thousand nations come together to admire*
> *   the City of Ten Thousand Buddhas.*

Therefore, everyone who comes to the City of Ten Thousand Buddhas is one of ten thousand Buddhas. Not only ten thousand Buddhas, but boundless Buddhas, innumerable Buddhas, peerless Buddhas, indescribable Buddhas, and *nayutas* of Buddhas. All of these inconceivable Buddhas will make their Bodhi resolve here and appear in the world.

我相信「門內有君子，門外君子至」，
萬佛城是萬佛所聚會的一個地方，
也就是世界所有的有智慧的人聚會的地方。
我常常說：萬佛城這兒，
無論哪一類的人到這兒，都是「英雄有用武之地」，
盡量發展你的抱負，只怕你沒有抱負；
你若有抱負，可以到這兒把它發揚光大，
共同給世界人類謀幸福。
我們要認識自己本來寶貴的自性，返本還原，
返迷歸覺，捨邪歸正，這就是萬佛城的宗旨。

I believe in the saying, "While there are men of virtue inside, men of virtue continue to arrive outside." The City of Ten Thousand Buddhas is a gathering place of ten thousand Buddhas. It is also a gathering place of wise individuals from all over the world. I often say, regardless of what kind of people come here, each one of them has his or her own talents. So, try to develop your aspirations to their fullest. The only thing to be afraid of is not having any aspirations. If you have aspirations, you can let them flourish here so that you can benefit everyone in the world. We must recognize our precious self-nature. Indeed, we should return to our original nature, from delusion to enlightenment, and from the heretical to the proper. These are the principles of the City of Ten Thousand Buddhas.

總而言之，你要知道在萬佛城不是很簡單的，
到了萬佛城都是有大因緣的；
不然的話，到不了的。
你看我們這些花草樹木都是在那兒說法，
這兒有飛禽、有走獸、又有在地裏住的眾生，
所謂飛、潛、動、植都有；
這很多種的動物裏邊，
也有菩薩化身在那兒教化眾生的。
菩薩是隨類示現的，
在哪一類眾生裏，
他就變化哪一類眾生的形，
去教化那一類的眾生。
眾生聽不聽他的教化，這又是一回事，
但是菩薩盡自己的心來教化眾生。

In short, you should know that it is not easy to be at the City of Ten Thousand Buddhas. In order to be here, there must be a deep affinity. If not, you will not even be able to get here. All of the flowers, grass and trees at the City of Ten Thousand Buddhas are speaking the Dharma. We also have birds, animals and all the various creatures who live in the ground. Among the various types of animals here, there are Bodhisattvas who manifest as animals in order to teach and transform living beings. Bodhisattvas can manifest in all manner of forms to accord with all types of living beings. In order to teach and liberate a particular type of living being, they can manifest in that particular form. If living beings will not listen to the Bodhisattvas' teachings, that is another matter. In any case, Bodhisattvas are committed to use all their resources to teach and liberate all living beings.

在一切花草樹木裏頭，也有樹神、花神，
在那兒給樹木花草說法，不過凡夫肉眼看不見，
就不知道這個妙處，不知道這種境界。
所以我們萬佛城這兒是天造地設的一個聖地。
這個聖地是幾萬萬年才出現一次，
而現在在西半球新大陸這塊土地上現出來了；
我說這話，你們不要當神話來聽，
這是實實在在地告訴你們，
認識不認識那是你們的事情了。

Among the vegetation, there are tree spirits and flower spirits speaking the Dharma for the trees, the flowers and the grasses. Because ordinary people cannot see them, they do not know about this ineffable place, this inconceivable state. The City of Ten Thousand Buddhas is a sagely place established by the ripening of causes and conditions. This kind of sagely place only appears once in thousands and thousands of years, and now it has appeared in the Western hemisphere, in this New World, on this site. Do not treat what I just told you as a myth. I have told you the truth, and it is up to you to understand. But I had to tell you!

萬佛城雖然
說是我用力量把它買下來的,
但是我還要聽從大家的意見。

我說過,萬佛城是全世界佛教徒的,
也是全世界人類的,也是全世界所有的眾生的。
為什麼我要說這種話?
我想修道的人不應該有自私心,
萬佛城是美國一塊寶貴的土地,
美國是一個領導世界的國家,
萬佛城是萬佛共同修道的地方。
共同修道的地方就不應該有自私心,
所以我要把它奉獻給全世界所有的眾生、所有的人類!

Although the City of Ten Thousand Buddhas was bought through my efforts, I still want to listen to everyone's ideas. I have said that the City of Ten Thousand Buddhas belongs to all Buddhists in this world, to all people in this world, and to all living beings in this world. Why do I say this? Because cultivators of the Way should not be selfish. The City of Ten Thousand Buddhas is a precious property on the American soil. America is a leader among the world's nations, and the City of Ten Thousand Buddhas is a place where ten thousand Buddhas gather to cultivate. Accordingly, there should not be any selfish thoughts at a place where all gather to cultivate. Therefore, I offer the City to all mankind and all living beings in this world!

因為萬佛城是世界佛教的一個道場，
也是世界的佛教發源地，
也是世界人類、佛教人類共同的歸宿處、
共同的皈依處，
所以我們在萬佛城用功修行的人，
一定要腳踏實地，老老實實地拿出一份真心來用功。
萬佛城現在等著人開悟，
等著人證果，等著人真正來修行。
萬佛城就是正法的一個開始，
萬佛城就是人人成佛的一個開始、一個道場，
所以到了萬佛城，決定要成佛！

CTTB

The City of Ten Thousand Buddhas is a Way-place for Buddhism all over the world. It is also the source of Buddhism in this world, a home and a sanctuary for all Buddhists and followers of all religions. Therefore, at the City of Ten Thousand Buddhas, we need to cultivate with diligence, honesty, dedication, and sincerity. The City of Ten Thousand Buddhas is waiting for people to come and cultivate, to attain the fruits of various stages of cultivation, and to attain enlightenment. The City of Ten Thousand Buddhas is a starting point for the Proper Dharma, and a starting point for everyone to obtain Buddhahood. Therefore, if you come to the City of Ten Thousand Buddhas, you must be determined to become a Buddha!

宣化上人簡傳

來自白雪皚皚的中國東北長白山區。
十九歲出家修道，發願普度一切眾生。
一九六二年將正確真實的佛法，
由東方帶到西方——美國。
創美國佛教史始有僧相之記錄——
一九六八年五位美國人在上人座下出家，
是在西方建立三寶的第一人。
「美國法界佛教總會」創辦人，
分支道場遍佈美、加、亞地區。
建立美國第一座佛教大道場——萬佛聖城。
一九九五年圓寂，「我從虛空來，回到虛空去」。
終其一生儘量幫助世界走向安樂光明的途徑，

A Brief Introduction to the Venerable Master Hsuan Hua

He came from the snow-laden vicinity of the Eternally
   White Mountains in northeastern China.
At the age of nineteen, he became a Buddhist monk
   and vowed to save all living beings.
In 1962, he brought the Proper Buddhadharma from East to West.
In 1968, five Americans took monastic vows under his guidance;
   thus, he established the Sangha and the Triple Jewel on American soil.
He founded the Dharma Realm Buddhist Association,
   with branch monasteries in the United States, Canada, and Asia.
He established the City of Ten Thousand Buddhas,
   the first large American Buddhist monastic community
In 1995,   before he passed into stillness, he said,
   "I came from empty space, and to empty space I will return."
Throughout his life, he promoted peace and light in the world,
   compassionately and tirelessly rescuing living beings.

法界 佛教總會簡介

- 創辦人宣化上人。
- 以法界為體,將佛教的真實義理,
  傳播到世界各地為目的;
  以翻譯經典、弘揚正法、
  道德教育、利樂一切有情為己任。

‧ 以不爭、不貪、不求、不自私、不自利、不妄語為宗旨。

‧ 有萬佛聖城等近三十座道場，遍佈美、亞洲；
　其僧眾均須恪遵佛制：日中一食、衣不離體，
　持戒念佛，習教參禪，和合共住，獻身佛教。

‧ 有國際譯經學院、法界宗教研究院、僧伽居士訓練班、
　法界佛教大學、培德中學、育良小學等機構。

‧ 本會道場、機構，門戶開放，凡各國各教人士，
　願致力於仁義道德、明心見性者，歡迎前來共同研習！

DRBA

An Introduction to the Dharma Realm Buddhist Association (DRBA)

- Founder: Venerable Master Hsuan Hua
- Taking the Dharma Realm as its substance, DRBA seeks to disseminate the true principles of Buddhism to all areas f the world. Its missions are to translate the Buddhist scriptures, to propagate the orthodox Dharma, to promote ethics-based education, and to benefit all sentient beings.

- The guiding principles of DRBA are: no contention, no greed, no seeking, no selfishness, no self-seeking, and no lying.
- In addition to the City of Ten Thousand Buddhas, DRBA has nearly thirty branch monasteries located throughout the United States, Canada, Asia, DRBA'S Sangha members honor the rules and practices established by the Buddha: eating only one meal a day, always wearing the precept sash, observing the precepts and being mindful of the Buddha, studying the teachings, practicing meditation, living together in harmony, and dedicating their lives to Buddhism.
- DRBA'S institutions include the International Institute for the Translation of Buddhist Texts, the Institute for World Religions, the Sangha and Laity Training Programs, Dharma Realm Buddhist University, Developing Virtue Secondary School, and Instilling Goodness Elementary School.
- The doors of DRBA's monasteries and institutions are open to anyone from any country who wishes to devote themselves to the pursuit of humaneness, justice, and ethics, and the discovery of their true mind.

金輪聖寺 Gold Wheel Monastery
235 North Avenue 58, Los Angeles, CA 90042 USA Tel: (323) 258-6668 Fax: (323) 258-3619

長堤聖寺 Long Beach Monastery
3361 East Ocean Boulevard, Long Beach, CA 90803 USA   Tel/Fax: (562) 438-8902

福祿壽聖寺 Blessings, Prosperity, and Longevity Monastery
4140 Long Beach Boulevard, Long Beach, CA 90807 USA Tel/Fax: (562) 595-4966

華嚴精舍 Avatamsaka Vihara
9601 Seven Locks Road, Bethesda, MD 20817-9997 USA Tel/Fax: (301) 469-8300

金峰聖寺 Gold Summit Monastery
233 First Avenue, West, Seattle, WA 98119 USA   Tel: (206) 284-6690

金佛聖寺 Gold Buddha Monastery
248 E. 11th Avenue, Vancouver, B.C. V5T 2C3 Canada
Tel: (604) 709-0248 Fax: (604)684-3754

法界佛教總會 · 萬佛聖城 Dharma Realm Buddhist Association & The City of Ten Thousand Buddhas
4951 Bodhi Way, Ukiah, CA 95482 USA
Tel: (707) 462-0939 Fax: (707)462-0949
http://www.drba.org , www.drbachinese.org

國際譯經學院 The International Translation Institute
1777 Murchison Drive, Burlingame, CA 94010-4504 USA
Tel: (650) 692-5912 Fax: (650)692-5056

法界宗教研究院 (柏克萊寺) Institute for World Religions (Berkeley Buddhist Monastery)
2304 McKinley Avenue, Berkeley, CA 94703 USA
Tel: (510) 848-3440 Fax: (510)548-4551

金山聖寺 Gold Mountain Monastery
800 Sacramento Street, San Francisco, CA 94108 USA
Tel: (415) 421-6117 Fax: (510)788-6001

金聖寺 Gold Sage Monastery
11455 Clayton Road, San Jose, CA 95127 USA
Tel: (408) 923-7243 Fax: (408)923-1064

法界聖城 City of the Dharma Realm
1029 West Capitol Avenue, West Sacramento, CA 95691 USA
Tel: (916) 374-8268 Fax: (916)374-8234

華嚴聖寺 **Avatamsaka Monastery**
1009 4th Avenue S.W., Calgary, AB T2P 0K8 Canada
Tel: (403) 234-0644 Fax: (403)263-0637

金岸法界 **Gold Coast Dharma Realm**
106 Bonogin Road, Mudgeeraba, Queensland
4213, Australia
Tel: (07) 5522-8788 Fax (07) 5522-7822

法界佛教印經會 **(**美國法界佛教總會駐華辦事處**)**
Dharma Realm Buddhist Books Distribution Society
臺灣省臺北市忠孝東路六段 85 號 11 樓
11th Floor, 85 Chung-hsiao E. Road, Sec. 6, Taipei,
Taiwan, R.O.C.
Tel: (02) 2786-3022, 2786-2474 Fax: (02) 2786-2674

法界聖寺 **Dharma Realm Sagely Monastery**
臺灣省高雄縣六龜鄉興龍村東溪山莊 20 號
 Tel: (07) 689-3713 Fax: (07)689-3870

彌陀聖寺 **Amitabha Monastery**
臺灣省花蓮縣壽豐鄉池南村四健會 7 號
Tel: (03) 865-1956 Fax: (03)865-3426

佛教講堂 **Buddhist Lecture Hall**
香港跑馬地黃泥涌道 31 號 11 樓
31 Wong Nei Chong Road Top Floor, Happy Valley,
 Hong Kong, China
Tel: (2)2572-7644 Fax: (2)2572-2850

般若觀音聖寺 (紫雲洞)
Prajna Guan Yin Sagely Monastery
(Formerly Tze Yun Tung Temple) Batu 5 1/2,
Jalan Sungai Besi, Salak Selatan,
57100 Kuala Lumpur, West Malaysia
Tel: (03)7982-6560 Fax: (03)7980-1272

法界觀音聖寺 (登彼岸) **Kun Yam Thong Temple**
(Formerly Deng Bi An Temple)
161, Jalan Ampang, 50450 Kuala Lumpur,
Malaysia
Tel: (03) 2164-8055 Fax: (03) 2163-7118

蓮華精舍 **Lotus Vihara**
136, Jalan Sekolah, 45600 Batang Berjuntai,
Selangor, Malaysia Tel: (03) 3271-9439

法緣聖寺 **Fa Yuan Sagely Monastery**
1, Jalan, Utama, Taman Serdang Raya,
43300 Seri Kembangan,Selangor, Malaysia
Tel: (03) 8948-5688

馬來西亞法界佛教總會檳城分會
Malaysia Dharma Realm Buddhist
Association Penang Branch
No. 32-32C, Jalan Tan Sri Teh Ewe Lim, 11600
Jelutong,Penang, Malaysia
Tel: (04) 281-7728, Fax: (04) 281-7798

TEN THOUSAND BUDDHAS CITY

ACCOMPLISHES

TEN THOUSAND BUDDHAS

出版日 西曆二○一○年十一月十日・初版三刷
　　　 佛曆三○三七年十月五日・達摩祖師誕辰 恭印

作　者 宣化上人
發行人 法界佛教總會・佛經翻譯委員會・法界佛教大學
地　址 **Dharma Realm Buddhist Association &**
　　　 The City of Ten Thousand Buddhas（萬佛聖城）
　　　 4951 Bodhi Way, Ukiah, CA 95482 U.S.A.
　　　 電話: (707) 462-0939　傳真: (707) 462-0949

出　版 法界佛教總會中文出版部
　　　 臺灣省臺北市忠孝東路六段 85 號 11 樓
　　　 電話: (02) 2786-3022　傳真: (02) 2786-2674

倡　印 法界佛教印經會（美國法界佛教總會駐華辦事處）
　　　 地址／電話：同上

　　　 法界文教基金會
　　　 臺灣省高雄縣六龜鄉興龍村東溪山莊 20 號
　　　 www.drbataipei.org／www.drba.org
　　　 ISBN:978-0-88139-869-4